PRAYING THE OUR FATHER IN LENT

Carl E. Olson

*All booklets are published
thanks to the generosity of the supporters
of the Catholic Truth Society*

Images: Page 4: *Agony in the Garden*, 1457-1459, by Andrea Mantegna. Musée Des Beaux-Arts, Tours. Photo by DeAgostini/Getty Images.

Page 53: *Saint Veronica* by Rogier van der Weyden. Kunsthistorisches Museum, Vienna. Photo by DeAgostini/Getty Images.

Page 71: *Christ Appearing to His Mother*, c.1496, by Juan de Flandes. The Bequest of Michael Dreicer, 1921. The Metropolitan Museum of Art.

All rights reserved. First published 2021 by The Incorporated Catholic Truth Society, 42-46 Harleyford Road, London SE11 5AY. Tel: 020 7640 0042 Fax: 020 7640 0046. © 2021 The Incorporated Catholic Truth Society. www.ctsbooks.org

ISBN 978 1 78469 653 5

Contents

PART ONE: LENT AND THE "OUR FATHER"

An Introduction 5

True Love Means Knowing His Name 11

The End is Here 17

Supernatural Will Power 23

Everlasting Daily Bread 29

Forgive, For Eucharist's Sake 35

Please, Don't Tempt Me! 41

Easter Delivers Us From Evil 47

PART TWO: PRAYING YOUR WAY THROUGH LENT

A Week-By-Week Scriptural Guide 54

Ash Wednesday 56

First Week of Lent 58

Second Week of Lent 60

Third Week of Lent 62

Fourth Week of Lent 65

Fifth Week of Lent 68

PART ONE

LENT AND THE "OUR FATHER"
An Introduction

*Ashes. Prayer. Fasting. Confession.
Supplication. Repentance.*

This is the language of Lent, that sacred time of reflection and self-examination, a forty-day journey into the desert. It begins on Ash Wednesday, when a charred cross is traced across our brows, a reminder of our mortality: "For you are dust, and to dust you shall return." That simple act is also a reminder that the brow of the Son of Man was marked with thorns and blood, with love and sacrifice. At Lent, the disciple is called to follow more closely in the steps of his master, to take up the cross, and to follow him into the wilderness in preparation for the Paschal Triduum.

Like Daniel, who longed to return to Jerusalem out of captivity in Babylon, the Christian begins the Lenten journey by seeking his maker and admitting his own unworthy state: "So I gave my attention to the Lord God to seek him by prayer and supplications, with fasting, sackcloth, and ashes." The journey to the New Jerusalem is marked and measured with prayer and confession: "We have sinned, committed iniquity, acted wickedly, and rebelled, even turning aside from thy commandments and ordinances" (*Dn* 9:3, 5).

This essential humility paves the path for holiness in the journey towards the heart of God. "Lent helps Christians to enter more deeply into this 'mystery hidden for ages' (*Ep* 3:9)," stated Pope St John Paul II in a Lenten Message in 2000. "It leads them to come face to face with the word of the living God and urges them to give up their own selfishness in order to receive the saving activity of the Holy Spirit." The mystery is met in the person of Jesus Christ, through whom the Christian has bold and confident access to the Father (*Ep* 3:11-12). The mystery is the Gospel, the good news of the God-man, sent by the Father to save those who are lost and who wander, in need of a shepherd. The mystery *is* Jesus.

Baptised by his cousin John in the Jordan River, the good shepherd was revealed as the beloved Son of the Father (*Mt* 3:16-17). Rising from the waters, Jesus was led immediately by the Spirit "into the wilderness to be tempted by the devil" (*Mt* 4:1). His forty days and nights revisited the forty years spent by the Israelites in the desert following their passage through the Red Sea. The three temptations Jesus faced were the same temptations faced by the chosen people of the Old Covenant: choosing physical comfort over obedience to God, loudly demanding God's miraculous intervention rather than quietly trusting in him, and attempting to succeed without suffering.

These ancient temptations are timeless, as attractive and deadly today as they were centuries ago.

His identity revealed and his public mission established, the Son's time in the desert was spent privately abiding in the presence of his Father. That sacred time was filled with prayer and fasting. Without prayer, Lent is a wasteland without relief and a journey without direction. "The journey to which Lent invites us takes place above all in *prayer*," John Paul II reminded the Catholic faithful in his 2001 Homily for Ash Wednesday. "Christian communities must become authentic 'schools of prayer' in these weeks." The greatest prayer of the Christian Faith – the Our Father – was given by Jesus in the midst of his sermon on the kingdom of heaven, the Sermon on the Mount (*Mt* 6:5-13).

The *Catechism of the Catholic Church* states that the Lord's Prayer is "the fundamental Christian prayer" (*CCC* 2759) and "the summary of the whole Gospel" (*CCC* 2761). As such, it teaches the Christian how to think, to live, and to be. "The Lord's Prayer is the most perfect of prayers," St Thomas Aquinas teaches, "In it we ask, not only for all the things we can rightly desire, but also in the sequence that they should be desired. This prayer not only teaches us to ask for things, but also in what order we should desire them" (*CCC* 2763). The Lord's Prayer places thoughts and desires in the proper order, focused first on the name, the kingdom, and the will of God, and then turning to our daily bread, forgiveness, and need for protection from temptation and evil.

Prayer and fasting are companions on the Lenten path. Fasting from bodily food during Lent, especially on Ash Wednesday, demands an increase in spiritual food. The hunger felt by the body should intensify the hunger felt for the Word of God, for Holy Communion, and for the presence of the Spirit. The work of the Son and the Holy Spirit is to bring hungering humanity to the Father, and the Our Father orientates the thirsting soul towards the Father's will and kingdom. Lent is an especially appropriate time to meditate on the prayer given us by Jesus, and to consider the holiness of God's name, the mystery of his kingdom, and the priority of his will. The petitions of the prayer are reminders that in the desert hunger increases ("give us this day our daily bread"), temptation grows ("lead us not into temptation"), and evil abounds ("deliver us from evil"), but for those who call upon their Father, there is nourishment, salvation, and solace. And for those who resist the devil, following the example of Jesus, there are angels waiting to minister (cf. *Mt* 4:11).

During these seven weeks of Lent we will contemplate the seven petitions of the Our Father, taking as our guide these words from the *Catechism*:

After we have placed ourselves in the presence of God our Father to adore and to love and to bless him, the

Spirit of adoption stirs up in our hearts seven petitions, seven blessings. The first three, more theological, draw us towards the glory of the Father; the last four, as ways towards him, commend our wretchedness to his grace. "Deep calls to deep" (*CCC* 2803).

From wretchedness to grace, from death to life, from the depths of death to the depths of life – these are beautiful descriptions of what Lent should be for the sons and daughters of God. Through Christ, those who accept the ashes on their heads will have their hearts filled with the divine life of God (cf. *2 P* 1:4). Led by the Holy Spirit, those who seek the Father through prayer and fasting will be made into "other 'Christs'" (*CCC* 2782), travelling towards the final Jerusalem that Daniel hoped to see. "Since the Lord's Prayer is that of his people in the 'endtime'," states the *Catechism*, the "our" in the Our Father also expresses "the certitude of our hope in God's ultimate promise: in the new Jerusalem he will say to the victor, 'I will be his God and he shall be my son'" (*CCC* 2788).

Reflection:

- The Our Father appears in Matthew 6 and Luke 11. The *Didache*, also known as *The Teaching of the Twelve Apostles* and one of the oldest non-canonical Christian writings, contains the instruction: "You should pray in this way three times a day" (8:3). Consider praying the Our Father three times a day (morning, noon, and evening) during Lent.

• The Lord's Prayer comes in the middle of the Sermon on the Mount (*Mt* 5-7). Jesus's central message in that great sermon was that the kingdom of heaven is at hand and how one must live in order to be part of it. Read Matthew 6 on Ash Wednesday and reflect on what Jesus teaches about these three key practices of the kingdom: almsgiving, prayer, and fasting.

• One of the challenges of our time is to present the truth about God the Father to people who don't know their earthly fathers or have poor relationships with them. Consider how your understanding of your heavenly Father has been shaped by your earthly father. Choose a quality of God the Father (e.g., mercy, love, justice, etc.) that you don't often think about or give thanks for and meditate upon it during the week.

True Love Means Knowing His Name

The 1970s rock band The Doors had a popular "love" song with the lyric, "Hello, I love you, won't you tell me your name?" If God had been the lyricist, "Hello, I love you, that's why I told you my name," would have been far, far better.

The Christian life, including Lent, is about true and eternal love, and true love longs to be in the presence of the one loved. So, when we pray the Our Father, we first place ourselves in his presence. This is what Jesus does when he journeys in the desert: "Filled with the Holy Spirit, Jesus returned from the Jordan and was led by the Spirit into the desert for forty days." If Lent is going to take us into a deeper relationship with the Father, we need to begin by first being in that relationship. It begins at baptism, but it will sometimes need to be restored through the sacrament of reconciliation. This is why Ash Wednesday focused so strongly on repentance and confession; its purpose was to reorientate us and prepare us for the forty days of Lent. Only after acknowledging our true relationship with God as needy sinners seeking his holiness can we can journey on to grow in that holiness and in our love for him.

That's one reason it is so fitting to contemplate the Our Father during Lent, for this great prayer of the Church is meant to guide us into holiness and spiritual growth. It does so by setting the proper priorities and lifting our heart and mind to heaven: "Our Father, who art in heaven." Then the first three petitions of the Our Father orientate us towards the Father: his name, his kingdom, and his will. The final four petitions focus on our relationship to Our Father, asking us to sustain us on our Lenten journey: asking for daily bread, forgiveness, protection from temptation, and deliverance from evil.

In this chapter we will examine the first petition of the Our Father: "Hallowed be thy name." The word "hallowed" is not one we hear in everyday conversation. Perhaps the only time we hear it out in the "real world" is at Halloween, or All Hallows Eve, when the Church celebrates the saints, who are "holy ones." *Hallowed* is the Old English word for "holy" or "sanctified." The ancient Hebrews recognised that a name is virtually the same as the thing or person being named. So they would not state his name, so immense was their respect for God's holiness.

As important as holiness is, we sometimes have an incomplete understanding of it. Often holiness is associated exclusively with moral purity and "being good." But we don't pray that God's name will be good or morally pure; rather, we express our desire that God's name will be set apart, that we will always keep it sacred, recognising that

God alone is worthy of worship. "We pray 'Hallowed by thy name,'" Cyprian writes, "not that we wish that God may be made holy by our prayers but that his name may be hallowed in us."

A literal translation of this phrase from the Our Father could be, "May Your name be sanctified." Only God is sanctified, holy, and complete in himself. Only those chosen by God to be set aside, or made holy, will be sanctified. Only those united to the Father, through the Son, in the power of the Holy Spirit, can be holy. "He has, however, willed to make men holy and save them," the *Catechism* explains, "not as individuals without any bond or link between them, but rather to make them into a people who might acknowledge him and serve him in holiness." This service is really about being in love with God, the God who is love and sent his Son for our salvation.

When we ask the Father that his name be hallowed, or holy, we enter more deeply into his plan of salvation for us, what the Catechism calls the "innermost mystery" of the Godhead and "the drama of the salvation of our humanity." In the tenth chapter of his Epistle to the Christians in Rome, quoting the prophet Joel, St Paul states, "For everyone who calls on the name of the Lord will be saved" (*Rm* 10:13). Salvation comes through Jesus Christ alone. "For God has not destined us for wrath," the Apostle told the Christians in Thessalonica, "but to obtain salvation through our Lord Jesus Christ" (*1 Th* 5:9). The holy name of God is fully revealed by Jesus; he gives it to us and sanctifies his own name so that we might also be consecrated, or made holy, for his work: "Holy Father…for their sake I consecrate myself" (*Jn* 17:19). Jesus alone, who is the Holy One of God, can call God "Father." United to Jesus, the holy ones of God can now call God "Our Father."

As Christians, we share in the name of the Christ – and in his holiness. And when we recognise and proclaim God's holiness, we promise to make his name and reputation holy here on earth. In praying "Hallowed be thy name," we swear an oath, out of love for the Father, to pursue holiness for his sake and for the sake of his Church. This requires hard work and training, trials and difficulties. It requires fasting and prayer. In other words, Lent is meant for this life-giving pursuit.

The uniqueness of Christianity is not primarily in its moral code, for we share many of the same essential moral and ethical beliefs as other religions. The heart of Christianity is ultimately not doing good things – as important as they are. It's in entering into intimate communion with that most loving of relationships, the Holy Trinity. Becoming holy and being a saint involves the complete gift of ourselves – body, soul, and spirit – to the One who gives himself completely to us – body, blood, soul, and divinity – in the Eucharist.

In a word, it's about love: true love, trinitarian love. God is love and holiness. God's holiness is at the "inaccessible centre of his eternal mystery," the *Catechism* states. A beautiful picture of this is found in *The Apocalypse*, the Revelation of Jesus Christ, which describes the throne room of God echoing with the great song of praise, "Holy, holy, holy is the Lord God Almighty, who was and who is and who is to come." The Psalmist sings, "Blessed be the name of the Lord from this time forth and forever." *There* is a song worth singing!

Reflection:

- God's name is holy, but do we sometimes treat it in an unholy manner? If you ever use God's name in vain, commit yourself this Lent to stop that habit. Perhaps you know someone or work with somebody who takes God's name in vain. Pray for that person and look for an opportunity to explain to them why their action bothers you.

- Being holy means being set apart by God to do his will and work. What specific work is God calling you to do during Lent? During this year? With your life? Ask God for growth in holiness and also for the ability to do what he desires of you.

- Ezekiel 1 and Revelation 4 offer powerful depictions of God's holiness and splendour. Read them and consider what being in the throne room of

God might be like. If you could see yourself from the vantage point of heaven, how might that affect your thoughts and actions?

• Romans 9-11 is one of the more difficult passages of the New Testament, but it is also – like Romans 10:8-13 – full of profound truths about confessing, believing, and calling on the name of the Lord. Contemplate that specific passage and what it means to carry out those three actions in the everyday world.

The End is Here

"We are living in the end times!" It's the sort of statement you might expect to hear from a televangelist or a street-corner preacher. "The end is near! The last days are upon us!" Such apocalyptic ideas are for fundamentalists and doomsday watchers, aren't they?

Not necessarily; the author of the epistle to the Hebrews writes that God "in these last days has spoken to us in his Son, whom he appointed heir of all things, through whom also he made the world." The *Catechism of the Catholic Church* in commenting on the Lord's Prayer states, "The end-time in which we live is the age of the outpouring of the Spirit." When did the outpouring of the Holy Spirit occur? At Pentecost, some two thousand years ago; so not only are we living in the end times, but so too were the Christians in the catacombs, in the medieval monasteries and in the seventeenth-century Vatican.

The Church does teach that there will be a final time of trial and that Christians living then will endure great tribulation and persecution: for Catholics, contemplating the "end times" is not primarily about finding out when, or even how, the world will end, but anticipating the full and final establishment of God's kingdom. So we pray, "thy kingdom come," three short words heavy with meaning, both for the present and for the future. The kingdom is a grand concept, a specific reality, and an ongoing activity – all at once; when we pray that the Father's kingdom will come, we recognise that Jesus established that kingdom during his first coming, that the kingdom is growing at this very moment, and that the kingdom will one day – at a time known only to God – be fully revealed in power and glory. This second petition of the Our Father has many meanings, primarily the return of Christ, when the one who established the kingdom will finish that work.

The Lord's Prayer, then, is a prayer for the final and glorious appearing of the kingdom. It is an anticipation of when Christ, crowned with thorns and crucified during his first coming, will return crowned with glory and revealed in all his majesty. This kingdom is the messianic kingdom, present in the person of Jesus, the Messiah. The Second Vatican Council teaches that, from the present time until the final hour, the church is a priestly kingdom "in which the kingdom of God is mysteriously present, for she is the seed and beginning of the kingdom on earth."

The Church – in other words the kingdom of Christ now present in mystery – grows visibly through the power of God in the world.

Meanwhile, we live in a state of tension between the first and second comings of our Lord. We are pilgrims on earth but also citizens of heaven, which means that there will always be some tension in our lives. John Paul II wrote quite vividly about this, specifically describing it as "eschatological tension," the tension caused by living in temporal history between the "already accomplished" – the Incarnation – and the "yet to be completed": the return of Christ and the fullness of the kingdom. This can be felt and experienced during Lent, when we seek to free ourselves, by God's grace, from the evil of this world while being witnesses to the Gospel in the world. While yet on earth, we live with the knowledge that we are meant for heaven. We understand that we are spiritual *and* material. We know that we are sinful *and* saved. We recognise that we are dying *and* graced with eternal life.

This can be either disconcerting or exciting, frustrating or encouraging, depending on how we choose to respond to it. We can always choose to ignore, or try to ignore, that The End will come for each and every one of us. We can choose to say, "*My* kingdom come," and seek to fulfil ourselves through material means, pursuing earthly pleasures without concern for eternity. Or we can say, "*Thy* kingdom come," and live in deeper communion with the Father. Lent is an aid in our quest to say this petition with our entire being. The acts of confessing, repenting, fasting, and giving are all meant to free us from unhealthy attachments and refocus our hearts and minds on the will of the Father and the reality of his kingdom.

One vital way to appreciate that reality better is to spend time before the Blessed Sacrament during Lent, to rest in the presence of the King. "The kingdom of God has been coming since the Last Supper," the *Catechism* reminds us, "and in the Eucharist, it is in our midst" (2816). The Eucharist, wrote John Paul II in his final encyclical *Ecclesia De Eucharistia*, is "a straining towards the goal, a foretaste of the fullness of joy promised by Christ; it is in some way the anticipation of heaven, the 'pledge of future glory'" (18). The King has come and he is with us, silently awaiting us, calling for us to spend time with him. He understands the tension in our lives and one day he will rid us of it. But for now it should drive us to him and – through him – to the fullness of the kingdom.

Unfortunately, there are many Christians, including some Catholics, who become obsessed with the end of time, their imaginations filled with bloody scenarios and violent visions. The incredible sales of apocalyptic themed fiction is evidence that people want to escape this world and flee from the temptations, difficulties, and trials that inevitably come our way; however, for disciples of the crucified King, escape is not a consideration and the cross cannot be avoided. If Lent tells us anything, it's that we must share in the sufferings of Christ. "Therefore do not be ashamed of the testimony of our Lord, or of me his prisoner," Paul exhorts Timothy, "but join with me in suffering for the gospel according to the power of God" (*2 Tm* 1:8).

Far from being reasons for despair, these sufferings and the tension of living in the present are reasons for hope. John Paul II explained:

> A significant consequence of the eschatological tension inherent in the Eucharist is also the fact that it spurs us on our journey through history and plants a seed of living hope in our daily commitment to the work before us. Certainly the Christian vision leads to the expectation of "new heavens" and "a new earth", but this increases, rather than lessens, our sense of responsibility for the world today (*Ecclesia de Eucharistia* 20).

The King is here. The kingdom is at hand. We *are* living in the end times.

Reflection:

- Jesus's forty days in the desert were part of his preparation for his ministry, which started not long after that time. Luke states that after undergoing his temptations, "Jesus returned to Galilee in the power of the Spirit" (*Lk* 4:14), and Matthew writes, "Jesus began to preach and say, 'Repent, for the kingdom of heaven is at hand'" (*Mt* 4:17). While Lent is a time of prayer and fasting, it is also a time of preparation – a time to get ready to declare the kingdom, in word and deed, in big ways and small ways, at every opportunity. In seeking God's grace to change our lives, we should also be preparing to change the lives of those around us. This doesn't mean making speeches, being confrontational, or handing out tracts, but being humble and peaceful in all that we do, being firm in our beliefs without needlessly upsetting others, and putting into practice the charity that God has given us. The proverb goes, "There is no Easter Sunday without Good Friday." The demands of Lent prepare us for the death of Good Friday; the darkness of Good Friday leads to the light of Easter morning.

Supernatural Will Power

It's natural to admire or be impressed by people with strong will power. We talk with respect about those special people who have "the will to succeed" and we often hear the optimistic saying, "Where there's a will, there's a way."

Will, as such, is not a bad thing; will is a God-given faculty we have by nature. It is what emables us to choose a course of action and make decisions. As we all know from experience, the will can choose good or evil; not only can we will to sin, we can completely forget – or ignore, as is usually the case – that *our* will is not the most important one in existence. That is why one reason the third petition of the Our Father – "Thy will be done on earth as it is in heaven" – is so helpful during Lent, a time that continually challenges us to choose between the perfect will of the Father and our imperfect will.

It's not by coincidence that Lent begins with a cross on Ash Wednesday and leads to the cross of Good Friday. The cross is all about the will; not about a will to succeed, or about exerting our own will power, but of surrendering our will to the Father. After all, no one gets up on a cross because they *feel* like it. No, they have to willfully choose to do so. Jesus is the perfect model of the surrender and trust required; he epitomises the humility demanded. Although the Son "existed in the form of God," Paul explains in his epistle to the Philippians, "he did not regard equality with God a thing to be grasped." Instead, he "humbled himself by becoming obedient to the point of death, even death on a cross" (*Ph* 2:7-8).

At the beginning of his ministry, during his forty days in the desert, Jesus rejected the temptations of Satan. Three years later at the end of his ministry, on the evening he would be betrayed in a garden, he again rejected the temptation to turn away from the Father's will: "My Father, if this cannot pass away unless I drink it, thy will be done" (*Mt* 26:42).

What was the Father's will for Jesus and what is it for us today? When we pray for the Father's will to "be done on earth as it is in heaven," what exactly are we asking for? Put simply, the redemption of creation and the salvation of man. In reciting the Our Father, the Church is praying that God will bring about the final completion of his plan of salvation. The Father's will is that "all men be saved" and "come to the knowledge of the truth" (*1 Tm* 2:3-4).

"What is God's will incarnated in Jesus?" asked Pope Francis in a 20th March 2019 general audience. "To seek and to save the one who is lost. And in prayer we ask that God's seeking may be successful, that his universal plan of salvation may be accomplished firstly in each of us and then in the entire world." God desires that no one should perish, but that all will know him. This certainly doesn't mean that man cannot reject God, or that there is no real judgement or hell. It does, however, make clear the depths of God's love for his wayward children and the lengths he will go to in order to save them.

The immeasurably deep and wide plan of the Father has been initiated through the Son, who in turn has entrusted its message to his body, the Church. "To carry out the will of the Father," stated the Second Vatican Council, "Christ inaugurated the kingdom of heaven on earth and revealed to us the mystery of that kingdom" (*Lumen Gentium* 3). Mankind now has access to the Father, through the crucified and resurrected Son, in the power of the Holy Spirit. We are now able to enter into God's will and, Peter states, become "partakers of the divine nature" (*2 P* 1:4). Heaven and earth – once separated by sin – are now joined by the Redeemer who is both God and man.

This wondrous plan of salvation is not just for us, our family, and a select group of friends, but is meant for the entire world. St Augustine states that we must pray for God's will to be accomplished in sinners also, not just in the saints. One way this happens, he explains, is by our prayers for our enemies. That's a truly Lenten task: how many of us naturally desire to pray for our enemies and hope for their salvation? How many of us, by our own strength, love those who annoy, irritate, anger, and frustrate us? Lent is a call to love; love is the heart of God and of his will. The *Catechism* remarks that the commandment to love one another as ourselves summarises all the other commandments "and expresses [God's] entire will" (*CCC* 2822).

To the world, the cross is an embarrassment and a scandal. To Christians, it is love in action. The world sees a dying, bloody man; we see the Son of God with open arms, reaching out to embrace the entire world in love – "on earth as it is in heaven." By gazing on the cross, our Lenten journey stays on course. By contemplating the sacrifice of our Saviour, we begin to comprehend the will of the Father and how to choose it. We are, the *Catechism* explains, "radically incapable" of surrendering our will with our own power, "but united with Jesus and with the power of his Holy Spirit we can surrender our will to him and decide to choose what his Son has always chosen: to do what is pleasing to the Father" (*CCC* 2825).

Any reflection on doing the Father's will would be lacking without considering Mary, the Mother of God. "Let it be to me according to your word," she said in complete obedience to the Father (*Lk* 1:38). She knows his will; she happily accepted her vital place and role in his plan of salvation, a perfect model for each of us. And she desires that we join her in handing our will over to the Father: "By entrusting ourselves to her prayer, we abandon ourselves to the will of God together with her" (*CCC* 2677).

In *The Great Divorce*, which describes eternal choices in a powerful fashion, C.S. Lewis wrote, "There are only two kinds of people in the end: those who say to God, 'Thy will be done'; and those to whom God says, in the end, '*Thy will be done.*'" Those are the choices. We can either thrive in the Lenten desert by embracing the Father's will, or we can destroy ourselves by pursuing mirages and dust devils. "The world is passing away, and also its lusts," the Apostle John observes, "but the one who does the will of God abides forever" (*1 Jn* 2:17). Now *that* is true will power.

Reflection:

- Each of us wants to know what God's will is for our lives. But how often do we think of God's will in terms of redemption and salvation? Are we open to sharing the gospel with friends and colleagues?

- Are we sometimes silent about our love for Jesus when someone mocks Christianity? This week, try to spend some time in prayer asking God to give you strength and encouragement in those situations. Consider how you can spread the Good News with those around you.

- Is there an area of your life that you still haven't given to God? If so, why not? What is holding you back from surrendering that part of your life to him?

Pray and meditate on the prayer of Jesus: "Father, not my will, but yours be done. Amen."

• Our Blessed Mother is always ready to pray for us and to lend her maternal aid. Make a list of Mary's qualities that you admire the most. Select one that you would like to grow in and ask her to pray for you and your growth in that regard.

Everlasting Daily Bread

Have you ever heard of the TANSTAAFL Principle? It's better known as the "There Ain't No Such Thing As A Free Lunch" principle. Its central premise is that everything worthwhile has a cost. There is a price for everything; there are no free meals or free rides. One of the great paradoxes of the Christian faith is that God's grace is a free gift, but accepting it costs us everything. We cannot earn God's love, but that love most certainly comes with a price. "For you have been bought with a price," the Apostle Paul wrote to the Corinthians, "therefore glorify God in your body" (*1 Co* 6:20). This important truth is at the heart of Lent, a time of counting the cost and glorifying God through our actions. We should be counting the cost of discipleship, of taking up the cross of Christ, and of dying to ourselves. We should be glorifying God by praying, fasting, and turning away from sin.

Looking at these actions through the lens of the fourth petition of the Our Father – "Give us this day our daily bread" – brings a deeper appreciation of the costs and benefits of being a Christian. We can also see how the practical concerns and challenges of this earthly life relate to the matters of eternal life. For the Christian, the earthly and heavenly are distinct but intimately related. This is the clear message of the Incarnation, from which the sacraments flow. God did not become man merely to save our souls, but also our bodies. Our citizenship is in heaven, but we are not angels or ghosts. We are an astounding, mysterious combination of both flesh and spirit. Therefore, on the physical level the request in the Our Father for daily bread is quite concrete, even practical. We need to eat in order to live. As children of our heavenly Father, we trust in him for the basic necessities of life: food, clothing, and shelter. Our fasting and giving during Lent remind us that these essentials should never be taken for granted and that there are many who do not possess them. The petition for daily bread is our prayer that all men and women will have meals to eat, clothing to wear, and homes to live in. Every moment of every day is a gift from God; taking this for granted eventually leads to ingratitude, which can lead to a hardened heart and arrogance.

Just as Lent points us to our eternal destination through temporal and material means, the Lord's Prayer also points us towards heavenly glory by way of earthly and even prosaic paths. The entire prayer is eschatological in nature – that is, it directs towards The End (the *eschaton*) and teaches us to think and pray as pilgrims on earth travelling towards heaven. Thus our daily bread is not just ordinary food, but the Bread of Life and the food of immortality, the Eucharist.

The Greek word *epiousios*, used for "daily" in the petition "give us this day our daily bread" has puzzled and fascinated scholars for centuries. It is a seldom-used word that possesses several levels of meaning. On one hand it refers to the here and "now", today's bread. It can also refer to the "bread needed to live." And it also can mean "bread for the coming day," a reference to a future heavenly life. The petition is a recognition that God provides food for our bodies *and* our spirits, that he meets us where we are at and provides the grace and sustenance to get where he wants us to go. "He who eats my flesh and drinks my blood has eternal life," Jesus declared to his startled disciples in his great Bread of Life discourse, "and I will raise him up on the last day" (*Jn* 6:54).

The destination on that last day is his kingdom, which is why the great Eastern Orthodox theologian Fr Alexander Schmemann described the Eucharist as "the sacrament of the kingdom of God." The sacraments, Schemann explained in his book *The Eucharist: The Sacrament of the Kingdom*, are eschatological in nature for they are "orientated towards the kingdom which is to come." They provide grace – the very life of God – without which we cannot have communion with him, or enter into the Beatific Vision. It's heady stuff, but the basic principle is simple: God provides us with the food for the journey. And while that food is a free gift, it does have a cost.

Part of the cost is the "eschatological tension" that we examined earlier. This tension is the result of our unique physical-spiritual make-up: we are on earth; we are meant for heaven; we are spiritual and material; we are sinful and saved; we are dying but filled with new life. Thankfully, the Son became man so that this tension could be addressed and resolved. Because the Son became man, men are now able to be sons of God. Because the divine became flesh, we who are flesh can now, Peter states, become "partakers of the divine nature" (*2 P* 1:4), for we truly are, as the Apostle John emphasised in his first Epistle, "children of God" (*1 Jn* 3:1-2).

The primary means by which the children of God on earth are prepared for heaven and the fullness of the kingdom is the Eucharist. This can be seen in the various ways the Eucharist is described. The *Catechism of the Catholic Church* describes it as the "pledge of glory" (*CCC* 1419) and "an anticipation of the heavenly glory" (*CCC* 1402). It is a true banquet; the Fathers of the Second Vatican Council taught that the Eucharist is "a meal of brotherly solidarity and a foretaste of the heavenly banquet" (*Gaudium et Spes*, 38). John Paul II, in his 2003 encyclical on the Eucharist in its relationship to the Church, painted this beautiful picture: "The Eucharist is truly a glimpse of heaven appearing on earth. It is a glorious ray of the heavenly Jerusalem which pierces the clouds of our history and lights up our journey" (*Ecclesia de Eucharistia* 19).

Lent is a mini-version of that lifelong journey. It helps us in comprehending the bigger picture by helping us get a grip on the pieces that make up that picture. These pieces include growth in patience, holiness, love, and self-control and the removal of selfishness, anger, lust, and bitterness. The daily bread of the Eucharist gives us the nourishment for growth and the strength to reject sin. It isn't a free meal, but it is a meal of freedom. "There is no surer pledge or dearer sign of this great hope in the new heavens and new earth 'in which righteousness dwells,' than the Eucharist," declares the *Catechism*. "Every time this mystery is celebrated, 'the work of our redemption is carried on' and we 'break the one bread that provides the medicine of immortality, the antidote for death, and the food that makes us live forever in Jesus Christ'" (*CCC* 1405).

Reflection:

- It's easy to take the basic necessities of life for granted and to forget about those who have to manage without them. Spend time this week thanking God for the food, clothing, and shelter he provides for you and your family, and pray for those who have less. Donate clothing, household items, or money to your local Catholic charity. Consider fasting an extra day as a reminder of your reliance on God's provision.

- In the book of Revelation John writes, "Blessed are those who are invited to the marriage supper of the Lamb" (*Rv* 19:9). Spend time before the Blessed Sacrament and contemplate the blessing of the Eucharist. Spend time thanking Jesus, the Bread of Life, for giving himself to the Church in such an incredible way.

- The Eucharist, St Augustine reminds us, creates a bond of union with all those who are members of Christ's body. If your relationship with a brother or sister in Christ is strained or in need of repair, take the steps necessary to restore the bond of union and love with them.

Forgive, For Eucharist's Sake

"To err is human, to forgive, divine." This well-known phrase, Monsignor Ronald Knox observed in *The Hidden Stream* (1952), captures two of the greatest mysteries of the Christian life: "That man, being what he is, can rebel against God; and the doctrine that God, being what he is, can forgive man." It also captures the essence of the fifth petition of the Our Father: "And forgive us our trespasses as we forgive those who trespass against us." Like the rest of the greatest prayer of the Christian Faith, it is deceptively simple. It's rather easy to pass over it and to think, "I know what that means: unless we forgive others, we won't be forgiven." If so, we risk turning it into a mere bargain or contract: I do this, this happens to me. To do so would be to sell short a deep reality.

Why? First, because being a child of God is not about bargaining or entering into a contract; it is about authentic love and participating in a covenant. The difference between a contract and a covenant is immense. A contract is a legal agreement that outlines how services are rendered and paid for. Complete strangers can make contracts with one another – and can fulfil those contracts perfectly without ever knowing the other party. But a covenant is a sacred and intimate union in which those involved give themselves completely to one another: body, soul, heart, and mind. If we break a contract, we can expect legal repercussions, but if we break a covenant we rupture a relationship. Put another way, and in the context of Lent, it is the difference between doing something out of obligation and doing it out of love. Do we give up a certain food or activity during Lent out of a sense of obligation, or out of love? Are we motivated by the desire to look good in the eyes of others, or by the desire to love God and know him more deeply? Are we fulfilling legal obligations owed to God or are we pursuing a relationship with our Father?

Seen in this light, the petition takes on a different and more profound shape. Far more than a balancing act, the *Catechism of the Catholic Church* tells us, "forgiveness is the fundamental condition of the reconciliation of the children of God with their Father and of men with one another" (*CCC* 2844). Forgiveness is at the heart of the new covenant, for without God's forgiveness man would remain alienated from him, and without our forgiveness of others we would not have communion with our brothers and sisters in Christ. So, forgiveness is always a gift from God; without his grace, we cannot forgive. This is why forgiveness is intimately linked to the fatherhood of God, something that can even be seen in the words of the Psalmist: "Just as a father has compassion on his children, So the Lord has compassion on those who fear him" (*Ps* 103:13).

There are two well-known parables of Jesus that articulate, in concrete terms, the Our Father's exhortation. One is the parable of the merciless servant (*Mt* 18:23-35), in which a slave who owes an unpayable sum of money to his master is forgiven that debt because of the master's compassion. Yet when that same slave then demands that a fellow slave who owes him a small sum pay it immediately or be thrown in prison, he fails completely to comprehend or consider the example of his master whose gracious compassion far exceeds the demands of justice and the law. The master, angered at the slave's evil action, throws him back into prison and punishes him again. Jesus states, "So shall my heavenly Father also do to you, if each of you does not forgive his brother from your heart." In the end, these relationships are familial; they are covenantal, not merely contractual.

The famous parable of the prodigal son (*Lk* 15:11-32) is even more familiar to us. The focus of commentaries and homilies is often on the son, who spurns his loving father and sets out to live a selfish life of pleasurable irresponsibility. But it is the love and mercy of the long-suffering father that is most striking; it could well be titled the parable of the long-suffering father. Having every right to be angry with his wayward son and to reject him, he instead runs to greet him upon his return home, embracing and kissing him in spite of his filthy ragged condition. And when the insolent "good" brother complains about this warm welcome he is met with perfect love: "My child, you have always been with me, and all that is mine is yours." The prodigal son, having been humbled and now filled with love, is restored to communion with his father; his brother, however, does not even address his father as "Father," portraying his lack of love. Although outwardly faithful, he severs that communion because he has been living in a contractual, not covenantal, relationship.

The ultimate goal of forgiveness is communion with God and with one another. It is no coincidence that this petition flows from the petition asking for daily bread. As we saw last week, one meaning of the fourth petition is a recognition and desire for the Eucharist, for Holy Communion. There are numerous connections to be made. Christ is the incarnation of forgiveness and to receive him in the Eucharist is to be flooded with the reality of forgiveness. In the Eucharist we receive the very body and blood of Christ, given for us on the cross for the forgiveness of sins. Receiving Holy Communion cleanses us of venial sins and helps to keep us from committing mortal sins. What is more, "asking forgiveness is the prerequisite for both the Eucharistic liturgy and personal prayer" (*CCC* 2631). The Eucharist provides the grace needed to forgive others and to embrace them as brothers and sisters even if our feelings and memories remain hurt by their actions.

Forgiveness, Romano Guardini remarked in his classic work *The Lord*, "is a part of something much greater than itself: love. We should forgive, because we should love." The covenantal communion that man has with God through Jesus Christ flows from the Communion of the Trinity, which is the "source and criterion of truth in every relationship" (*CCC* 2845). We will err – and others will err against us – because we are human. But we will also forgive, for we share in the divine life of God, who has forgiven us and made us his children.

Reflection:

- Lent is the perfect time to examine ourselves and see if we harbour resentment or ill will against someone: a family member, friend, colleague, neighbour, or fellow parishioner. Do we need to forgive them? Or is there someone we have offended or hurt, whose forgiveness we need to seek out? Consider making a list of people you are upset with or have ill feelings towards, and pray for them this week.

- "This petition is astonishing" states the *Catechism*; it is also the only petition that Jesus explains in more detail (see *Mt* 6:14-15). But it is also easy to overlook or pass over it with undue haste. If that has been the case for you, ask yourself why. Spend time this week reflecting on this petition and the parable of the prodigal son and his father.

• God's forgiveness can also easily be taken for granted. What would the world be like if the Father had not sent the Son to die for our sins? What would our lives be like if we had to live with our sins and guilt and had no way of dealing with them? What if we didn't have the Eucharist? Why not reflect on these questions before the Blessed Sacrament or while preparing for Mass.

Please, Don't Tempt Me!

The playwright and wit Oscar Wilde once wrote, "I can resist anything except temptation." The humour of the remark is mixed with a sad recognition that we fail so often to resist the temptations that come our way each day and from every direction. During Lent, the struggle against temptation and sin is, hopefully, brought into sharp focus. By simplifying our lives and removing distractions, hidden weaknesses are brought to light and sinful habits are recognised for what they are. The liturgies and devotions of the Lenten season help us to acknowledge our failings and our struggles with temptation. Times of prayer and contemplation lead us to ask hard questions: what are the temptations that confront us regularly? Why do we give in to them? What can we do to avoid occasions of sin? How must I change my ways in order to grow in holiness?

The sixth petition of the Our Father, at first glance, might not seem particularly helpful or even encouraging in these labours: "Lead us not into temptation…" This simple phrase has confused some Christians (and non-Christians) and has even proved scandalous to others: Does God *really* tempt us? Are we actually asking God not to tempt us?

Why would our loving Father, who cares for us and desires our everlasting communion with him, bring temptation into our lives?

Yes, this is a puzzling and difficult petition, but, as Cardinal Newman once noted, a thousand difficulties do not make a doubt. Part of the difficulty of this little phrase, the *Catechism of the Catholic Church* points out, is that the Greek word for "lead" is not easily translated into one English word. A better translation would be "do not allow us to enter into temptation," or "do not let us yield to temptation" (*CCC* 2846).

In this life, temptation is inevitable, but our prayer is that God will provide the wisdom to recognise it and the strength necessary to resist it when it comes. St James writes that the man who resists temptation is blessed and he will be given the crown of life – that is, eternal life; he makes it clear that temptation does not come from God: "Let no one say when he is tempted, 'I am being tempted by God'; for God cannot be tempted by evil, and he himself does not tempt anyone" (*Jm* 1:14-15).

Still, while God does not tempt us in the sense of enticing us to sinful acts, he does subject us to trials and difficulties; he tests us; he allows sickness, loss of reputation, persecution, tragedy, and poverty. Why? The *Catechism* states that it is because "filial trust is tested – it proves itself – in tribulation" (*CCC* 2734). Those dark and trying moments are when our trust, love, and dependence upon God are strengthened. It's easy to trust and love, or say that we do, when life is good and we have few worries. However, holiness grows in the heat of the desert; righteousness shines brightest in the darkness of night. St James, at the very opening of his epistle, encourages his persecuted first-century readers by telling them, "Consider it all joy, my brethren, when you encounter various trials" (*Jm* 1:2). Likewise, St Paul declares that "we also exult in our tribulations" (*Rm* 5:3) because they result in perseverance, a tested character and hope, all given by the Holy Spirit because of the love the Father has for his children.

The temptations and tests that we experience will either cause us to fall away or draw us closer to God; there is no neutrality. If we give in to temptation, especially on a regular basis, we will become deformed in spirit. Overcoming temptation by God's grace and our active free will conforms us to the likeness of Jesus. He is our model for resisting temptation and overcoming trials.

Jesus overcame temptation and the tempter, in the desert and in the garden, through prayer. "Pray that you may not enter into temptation," he exhorted the disciples. "Keep watching and praying," he tells them, "the spirit is willing, but the flesh is weak" (*Mt* 26:41). We must be vigilant and always aware of the dangers around us – and within us. Foremost is pride, which reveals itself in all sorts of ways: boasting, anger, gossip, and lack of charity.

Fasting helps to heighten our awareness of the temptation to commit such sins; our hunger reminds us that mere bread will not keep us alive, but that we need the Bread of Life. It helps us see that not all that tastes good – whether physically, intellectually, or emotionally – leads to life, but can sometimes lead to sin and death.

In the face of such dangers, Scripture assures us that our Father will not allow us to be tempted by Satan anymore than we can endure. "No temptation has overtaken you but such as is common to man," Paul writes, "and God is faithful, who will not allow you to be tempted beyond what you are able, but with the temptation will provide the way of escape also, that you may be able to endure it" (*1 Co* 10:13). The story of Job is an example of this truth; it is also a sobering reminder that the righteous do suffer and that those who love God will not necessarily avoid intense pain and suffering.

In addition to the daily temptations and trials that beset us, this petition also refers to the final trial, when apostasy and the spirit of the anti-Christ will assault followers of Christ with all the intensity that Satan can muster. In the Our Father we pray for the kingdom of God to come, and we pray to be spared from the time of testing that will precede it. The cosmic struggle between powers and principalities rages around us, even as we silently struggle in our hearts against the temptation to hurt, lust, hate, despise, ignore, and mistreat.

Lent reminds us – shows us, really – that those who embrace the Christ embrace his cross. We are promised a cross, and it is only with that promise that we have the hope of the resurrection. This "foolishness of God" (*1 Co* 1:25) is not easy to accept; sophisticated modern tastes see it as a stumbling block. For Christians, however, it is a source of hope and comfort. During those moments in the Lenten desert, we cling to the cross and remind ourselves that "I can do all things through him who strengthens me" (*Ph* 4:13). Jesus endured temptation and trial. He was mocked and beaten, stripped and killed. He was tested in every way that we are, "yet without sinning," declares the Epistle to the Hebrews (4:15). He resisted everything except love. By God's grace and for his glory, let us do the same.

Reflection:

- Spend some time examining your conscience and reflecting on practical ways that you can avoid temptation and occasions of sin. Are there patterns of your daily life that need to be changed? Are there places you need to avoid, or people you shouldn't spend time with? What about films, television shows or music you might watch or listen to? Are the books and magazines you read causing you to struggle with certain temptations?

- When Jesus goes into the desert and is tempted by Satan (*Mt* 4:1-17 and *Lk* 4:1-15), he rebukes him by quoting Scripture. Consider memorising some verses that remind you of God's faithfulness, that you can recite when you are tempted. Verses to consider memorising might include *1 Co* 10:13, *Heb* 2:18, or *Ps* 121 (120).

- There are several classic works of Catholic spirituality filled with encouragement and timeless practical advice about growing in holiness and dealing with temptation. Some of these works include *The Imitation of Christ* by Thomas à Kempis, *Introduction to the Devout Life* by St Francis de Sales, *The Spiritual Exercises of St Ignatius*, and *The Way of Perfection* by St Teresa of Avila. Consider reading one of these during the next few weeks or months, in combination with daily prayer and Bible study.

Easter Delivers Us From Evil

"Deliver us from evil."

Easter might not seem the right time to contemplate this final petition of the Our Father. After all, Easter is a time of joy and celebration, the Feast of feasts and, in the words of Athanasius, the Great Sunday.

Easter's joyful festivity is not due to some vague notion of being spiritually refreshed or the result of a community's desire to celebrate its ongoing existence. It is the proclamation that Jesus Christ did really suffer and die, that he destroyed the power of evil and the evil one, and that he is now truly risen from the dead. In the words of theologian Hans Urs von Balthasar, in his book *Mysterium Paschale*, "The whole New Testament is unanimous on this point: the cross and burial of Christ reveal their significance only in the light of the event of Easter, without which there is no Christian faith." This echoes Paul's blunt words to the Corinthians: "If Christ has not been raised, your faith is worthless; you are still in your sins" (*1 Co* 15:17).

To put it bluntly, Christianity without the cross is just another moral code taught by a great man, and the cross without the resurrection is just the tragic death of an inspiring leader.

The "evil" spoken of in the Lord's Prayer is not an abstract concept, but is better understood as the personification of evil: Satan. Belief in the existence of Satan is often mocked in our supposedly enlightened age (although Satan makes regular cameos on the big and small screen), even while the reality of evil can be seen all around the world in events monumental and minor: theft, murder, hatred, genocide, slavery, abuse, and corruption. The battle for souls rages around us, but the Risen Lord does not ask the Father to take us, his disciples, out of the world, but to keep us "from the evil one" (*Jn* 17:15). On our own we are incapable of grappling with Satan. He is a spiritual being – a fallen angel – whose intellect and power far exceeds that of any man. The lone exception is the God-man, who strengthens and protects his flock from evil (cf. *2 Th* 3:3).

"Faith in God the Father Almighty," states the *Catechism of the Catholic Church*, "can be put to the test by the experience of evil and suffering" (*CCC* 272). This is a lesson that many Christians learned during Lent, and one that others have experienced in dark moments of loneliness and hardship. At times it can seem that God is not there and that he cannot stop evil. Why did 9/11 happen? Why does the murder of millions of unborn babies continue? Where is God in the untimely death of the innocent and weak? Answers cannot be found apart from the Suffering Servant and the reality of Easter morning. "But in the most mysterious way God the Father has revealed his almighty power in the voluntary humiliation and resurrection of his Son, by which he conquered evil" (*CCC* 272). The resurrection confirms that Jesus is from God, and that the evil one and the power of death have been conquered. The difficulty, as we've seen before, is that we live between the cross and the return of the conquering King. We live in a battle zone, even though the final outcome is evident to those who enter into the Paschal Mystery at Easter. We are fighting the good fight, even though we endure while trusting the promise of resurrection and glory won by our Saviour.

The phrase "For Thine is the kingdom, and the power, and the glory, for ever. Amen" was added to Matthew's Gospel years after it was originally written. It was a formula used by the early Christians, and it appears in *The Didache*, or the Teaching of the Twelve Apostles, which was probably written around the end of the first century. It repeats the first three petitions of the Our Father: that his name be gloried, that his kingdom come in glory, and that the power of his will be known and accomplished.

The *Catechism* points out that the evil one, the ruler of this world, has "mendaciously attributed to himself the three titles of kingship, power, and glory" (*CCC* 2855). Satan wants to rule all things, to have power everywhere and over everything, and steal and destroy the glory of all that exists. This is the meaning of "anti-Christ": claiming for oneself all of the authority, power, and glory due to the true Christ. By his death and resurrection, Jesus destroys all of Satan's illusions, a reality powerfully depicted near the conclusion of the film *The Passion of the Christ* when Satan is shown howling in rage in the midst of a desolate landscape.

There is also a connection between this doxology, or "word of glory," and the three temptations that Jesus underwent in the desert before his public ministry began. Satan tempted Jesus to show his power by turning stones into bread. He tempted Jesus to reveal his heavenly glory by throwing himself from the top of the Temple and having angels carry him to safety. And the evil one offered Jesus all the kingdoms of the world if he would fall down and worship him. However, Jesus knew that his kingdom could only be established through suffering and death. He understood that true power comes through love and sacrifice, not fear and arrogance; he knew that his glorified body would result from rising from the grave, not by avoiding it. Jesus's rejection of Satan's temptations showed the heart of the Messiah who was intent on establishing his kingdom.

Now, on this side of Easter, we can see how Lent prepares us for that kingdom. Our time in the desert purifies us from the sins and attachments that keep us from holiness. The dark moments of temptation we face force us walk by faith, not by sight. United to Christ, we become more like him. Suffering with Christ, we learn to love truly. Dying with Christ, we learn to live truly. "Now if we have died with Christ," Paul writes, "we believe that we shall also live with him." United to his death, we share in his resurrected life: "For if we have become united with him in the likeness of his death, certainly we shall be also in the likeness of his resurrection."

Easter is the light at the end of the Lenten tunnel. The resurrection is the light that illuminates the entire liturgical year. By the resurrection the head of the evil one is crushed, the kingdom is established, and the children of God are made known. "The season before Easter signifies the troubles in which we live here and now," stated St Augustine in his homily on Psalm 148, "while the time after Easter which we are celebrating at present signifies the happiness that will be ours in the future." Amen.

Reflection:
• Lent is over, but you might want to take some time to think of what you learned during those forty days. What progress was made in your relationship with Jesus? What growth in holiness did you experience? How do you now plan to continue that growth? What distractions did you eliminate from your life? What

new habits did you start to establish and what will you do to make sure they continue?

• During the Easter season, look for opportunities to share the joy and hope that God has given you. Be aware of friends, family members or colleagues who need to be encouraged and be shown love in some way, big or small. God has given us the gift of his Son and of eternal life: what gifts can we give to those around us who are in need?

• In the Eastern tradition the following lines are sung repeatedly during Easter, "Christ is risen from the dead! By death he conquered death, and to those in the graves he granted life." In your personal prayer time, specifically thank Jesus for becoming man, suffering, and dying for you so as to break death's power over you. Thank him for the resurrection and for the resurrection he has made possible for those who are united to him. Thank him for conquering evil and for breaking the hold that the evil one had on the world. Praise him for his selfless love and sacrifice.

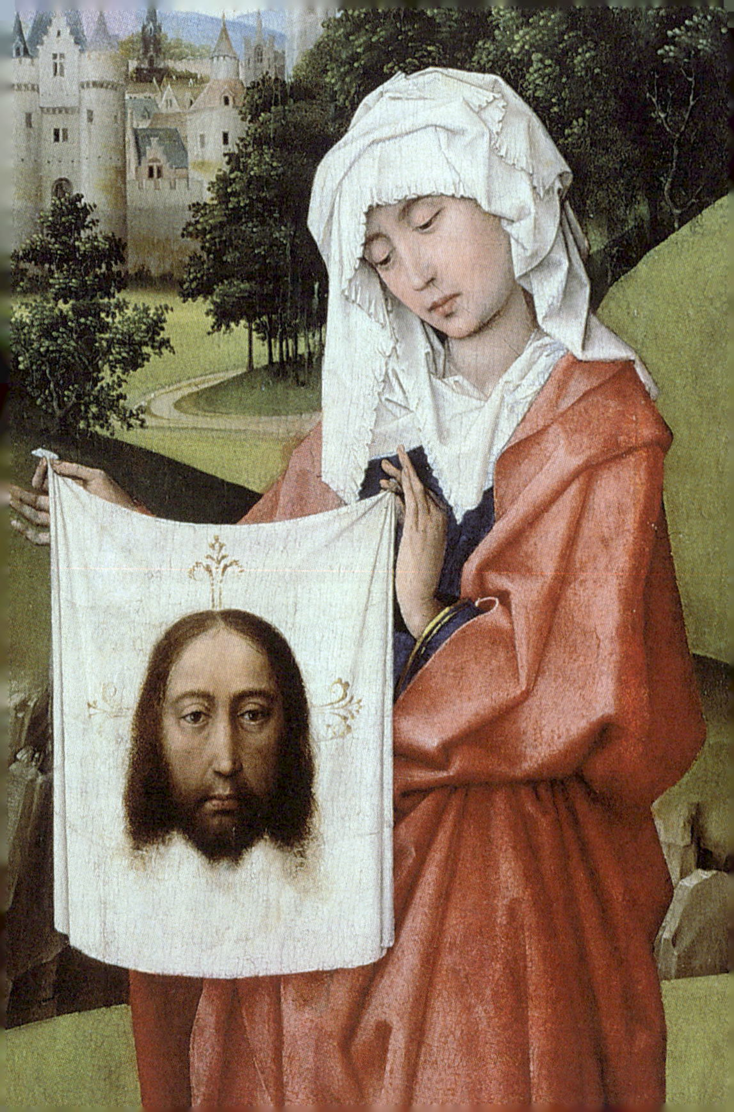

PART TWO

PRAYING YOUR WAY THROUGH LENT

A Week-By-Week Scriptural Guide

The journey of Lent, as we've seen, is one of love, a pilgrimage towards the profound and joyful mystery of the passion, death, and resurrection of Jesus Christ. That journey begins in the wilderness. "By the solemn forty days of Lent the Church unites herself each year to the mystery of Jesus in the desert" (*CCC* 540). As Benedict XVI stated in his first Lenten message, in 2006:

> Lent is a privileged time of interior pilgrimage towards him who is the fount of mercy. It is a pilgrimage in which he himself accompanies us through the desert of our poverty, sustaining us on our way towards the intense joy of Easter.

What follows is a scripture-based guide to praying during Lent, drawing on the readings for Ash Wednesday and the five Sunday of Lent from all three Cycles (A, B, and C). Each short reflection is meant for personal contemplation and prayer, and to accompany the public, communal, and liturgical prayers of the Church, all of which are ultimately focused upon and find their deepest meaning in the Eucharist, "the source and summit of the Christian life" (*CCC* 1324).

Key themes and ideas from each week of Lent are given, drawn from the readings, as well as a prayer selected from Tradition that can be prayed during that specific week.

Ash Wednesday

Themes: Repentance, Fasting, Mercy, Salvation, Following Christ, Prayer

"For our sake he made him to be sin who did not know sin," states the epistle for Ash Wednesday, "so that we might become the righteousness of God in him" (*2 Co* 5:21). The perfect Son, who is God, willingly became man and entered the fallen world so that sinful men and women might become children of God. This divine paradox echoes the remarkable words of Jesus: "For whoever wishes to save his life will lose it, but whoever loses his life for my sake will save it" (*Lk* 9:22-25). Lent is a season for seeing the world through the eyes of Christ, which means many of our assumptions will be challenged or even turned upside down. Prayer is essential for this new way of seeing what is really and truly living what we see in Christ. In the Gospel for Ash Wednesday, from the Sermon on the Mount, Jesus condemns those who give alms in order to gain attention, who pointedly appear gloomy while fasting to appear pious, and who pray in public in a way meant to garner praise. "But when you pray," Jesus said, "go to your inner room, close the door, and pray to your Father in secret. And your Father who sees in secret will repay you" (*Mt* 6:6).

After all, the call to follow Jesus is not meant for those who think they are already saved and spiritually whole. It is for those who desire to be truly alive and awake. Giving up food can sharpen this holy desire. "Fasting wakes us up," said Pope Francis in his 2018 lenten message. "It makes us more attentive to God and our neighbour. It revives our desire to obey God who alone is capable of satisfying our hunger."

Prayer

O Lord and Master of my life, take from me the spirit of sloth, despair, lust for power, and idle talk; give me in their place the spirit of chastity, humility, patience, and love for thy servant. Yea, O Lord and King, grant me to see my own transgressions, and not to judge my brother, for blessed art thou, unto ages of ages. Amen.

LENTEN PRAYER OF ST EPHREM

First Week of Lent

Themes: Temptation, Sin, The Fall, Prayer, Testing, Self-sacrifice, Perfection

The Gospel readings (from Matthew, Mark, and Luke, as John does not have an account of Jesus's forty days in the desert) for the first Sunday of Lent presents Jesus's dramatic confrontation with the devil. The three temptations that Jesus underwent in the wilderness represented three key temptations the Israelites had failed to overcome while they waited in the desert for forty years. The forty days and nights that Jesus spent in the desert represent those long years; likewise, the forty days of Lent are based upon the fast of our Lord, drawing us into the mystery of that sojourn: "By the solemn forty days of Lent the Church unites herself each year to the mystery of Jesus in the desert" (*CCC* 540).

Led by the Spirit and guided by the Church, we enter into a desert of sorts, renouncing various comforts and making more time for prayer and self-sacrifice. We contemplate the truth about sin and salvation; we test our hearts and ask: how do I use my freedom? Do I trust in God? How can I grow in obedience and love?

Also note that Jesus, after completeing his time in the desert, embarks upon his public ministry. Having spent time in solitude and prayer, he turns towards a life among the multitudes preaching and teaching. What is his core message? "The time is fulfilled, and the kingdom of God is at hand; repent, and believe in the gospel" (*Mk* 1:15). Lent, then, impresses upon us that the time is now, the kingdom is here, repentance is needed, and belief is imperative.

Prayer

Grant me, O Lord, to know what I ought to know, to love what I ought to love, to praise what delights thee most, to value what is precious in thy sight, to hate what is offensive to thee. Do not suffer me to judge according to the sight of my eyes, nor to pass sentence according to the hearing of the ears of ignorant men; but to discern with a true judgement between things visible and spiritual, and above all, always to inquire what is the good pleasure of thy will.

THOMAS À KEMPIS (1380-1471)

Second Week of Lent

Themes: Transfiguration, Glory, Calling, Blessing, Mercy, Purity, Humility, Trust

It might seem odd that the Transfiguration is so prominent during Lent (*Mt* 17:1-9; *Mk* 9:2-10; *Lk* 9:28-36), but it is a reminder that the goal of eternal glory is worth the trials, struggles, and moments of darkness. In the days leading up to the Transfiguration, Jesus had directly confronted and demolished any false notions the disciples might have had about the nature of his mission. He strongly expressed the unwavering commitment he had to offering himself as a sacrifice for the world: his kingdom was not of this world, and he was not a political leader or a military warrior; he was not promising comfort and wealth. On the contrary, Jesus was promising a cross.

Jesus took Peter, James, and John up Mount Tabor in order to call them to deeper discipleship, to a better understanding of Jesus's identity and calling, and a clearer knowledge of their own identity and calling. They were already blessed, but their blessing was to come to fullness by the way of the cross, for the cross is the doorway to communion with God. The Transfiguration was a foretaste of the power and glory of God; it was a grace meant to shine in the dark night that enveloped the apostles following the crucifixion. By contemplating the Transfiguration, we can give thanks for the revelation of God's glory, as well as for the trials and challenges that we must overcome, by God's grace.

Contemplate, then, this statement of the Father on the mountain: "This is my beloved Son, with whom I am well pleased; listen to him." *Listen to him.* Ponder the words of Christ. Gaze upon the Christ who is the Word!

Prayer

O St Joseph, whose protection is so great, so strong, so prompt before the throne of God, I place in thee all my interests and desires. O St Joseph, assist me by thy powerful intercession and obtain for me all spiritual blessings through thy foster Son, Jesus Christ Our Lord, so that, having engaged here below thy heavenly power, I may offer thee my thanksgiving and homage.

O St Joseph, I never weary contemplating thee and Jesus asleep in thine arms. I dare not approach while he reposes near thy heart. Press him in my name and kiss his fine head for me, and ask him to return the kiss when I draw my dying breath.

St Joseph, patron of departing souls, pray for me.

ANCIENT PRAYER TO ST JOSEPH

Third Week of Lent

*Themes: Commandments, Thirst, Faith, Hope, Love,
Living Water, Healing, Cleansing, Deliverance*

The readings during Lent often present us with encounters between God and man, and each of these sheds light on our own relationship with God. In Cycle C, there is the famous account of Moses and the burning bush (*Ex* 3:1ff), in which the banished shepherd engages in conversation with the God of Abraham, Isaac, and Jacob. God finally reveals his divine name, saying, "I AM WHO I AM," before promising liberation for the people of Israel from captivity in Egypt.

Several chapters later we find, in the Old Testament reading for Cycle A, that the people are grumbling and murmuring. Having already forgotten the saving work of God, they are so angry that Moses fears they will stone him. How, we wonder, could they be so forgetful and ungrateful? Yet if we are honest we recognise that we aren't any better: we've been baptised and liberated from sin, but we still complain. Perhaps we've had thoughts similar to what the people said to Moses: "But you had to lead us into this desert to make the whole community die of famine!" (*Ex* 16:3). Maybe we've also wondered, "Why did you ever make us leave Egypt?" (*Ex* 17:3). We find ourselves thinking with nostalgia about certain sins and temptations. Our faith wavers; our hope bends; our love wilts. We might even be tempted to blame God for our struggles with sin.

Then, in Cycle B, the Gospel is of Jesus cleansing the Temple with dramatic zeal before making the equally dramatic declaration: "Destroy this temple, and in three days I will raise it up" (see *Jn* 2:13-25). The Temple in Jerusalem, which was a place of worship and God's dwelling place among his chosen people, was becoming a place of corrupt commodity. Likewise, our daily lives can become compromised and even corrupted; we can start to accept failure and even sin as the norm. There has to be a reckoning and a cleansing. Our bodies, which are temples of the Holy Spirit (*1 Co* 6:19-20), need to be once again offered to God as a "living sacrifice" (*Rm* 12:1), so we can love, know, and worship God with everything we are.

Lent, then, can and should reveal the fragility of our faith, the frailty of our hope, the feebleness of our love. We might be tempted to blame God for our struggles with sin; worse, we may long for the comfort of sinful habits. It may seem easier to return to the slavery we know than to journey in faith towards the kingdom of God. But the burning fire of God's perfect love can cleanse us, opening our hearts to the joy and gratitude befitting true sons and daughters of God.

Prayer

Heavenly King, Comforter, Spirit of Truth, who art everywhere present and fill all things; Treasury of Blessings, and Giver of Life, come and dwell within us, cleanse us of all stain, and save our souls, O Gracious Lord. Amen.

"Heavenly King", Byzantine Prayer

Fourth Week of Lent

Themes: Light, Darkness, Blindness, Sight, Signs, Life, Death, Healing, Judgement, Resurrection

From the fourth Sunday of Lent until the end of the Lenten season, nearly all of the Gospel readings for each day are from the Gospel of John. The fourth Gospel has several great themes that are unique to it, including that of light and darkness, which is set forth in the prologue (*Jn* 1:1-18). "What came to be through him was life," the Apostle John wrote, "and this life was the light of the human race; the light shines in the darkness, and the darkness has not overcome it" (*Jn* 1:3b-5). This contrast is certainly evident in the Gospel reading for Cycle A, the account of the man born blind. The man, who was blind from birth, knows very little until he encounters the healing Saviour and is cured of both physical and spiritual blindness.

"This blind man," commented St Augustine on this story, "is the human race." Every one of us is born into spiritual blindness, recipients of the original sin and the severed communion between God and man going back to Adam. Each of us, like the blind man, is unable to heal ourselves; desiring to see, we stumble about in darkness and misery. We are in need of Christ and his light, which comes through his word and the sacrament of baptism. Lent is a good time to offer thanks for the gift of spiritual sight, and to go to Confession to confess any sins, mortal or venial, that have either destroyed or damaged the life of grace.

In the account of Nicodemus visiting Jesus by night (*Jn* 3:14-21), read in Cycle B, Jesus states that "everyone who does evil hates the light and does not come to the light lest his deeds should be exposed. But he who does what is true comes to the light, that it may be clearly seen that his deeds have been wrought in God." Entering the light of God – that is, conversion! – requires humility. And in the Gospel of Cycle C, the parable of the Prodigal Son (*Lk* 15) offers one of the most beautiful accounts of both humility – on the part of the wayward son who returns home – and profound forgiveness – on the part of the merciful father.

Forgiveness, Mgr Romano Guardini wrote in his classic book *The Lord*, "is a part of something much greater than itself: love. We should forgive, because we should love." Forgiving is difficult, and so is fighting temptation. As we pray throughout Lent, hidden weaknesses will come to light and sinful habits will reveal themselves. Times of prayer and contemplation lead us to ask hard questions: what are the temptations that regularly confront us? Why do we give in to them? What can we do to avoid occasions of sin? How must I change my ways in order to grow in holiness?

Prayer

Hail Mary, Full of Grace, The Lord is with thee. Blessed art thou among women, and blessed is the fruit of thy womb, Jesus. Holy Mary, Mother of God, pray for us sinners now, and at the hour of our death.

Fifth Week of Lent

Themes: Death, Resurrection, Mercy, Hypocrisy, Worship, Trust, God's Word, Faith

In the final week of Lent, death confronts us squarely. Ever since the Fall, death has been the enemy, the constant source of pain, despair, sadness, and woe. People seek to battle death in a million ways, all of them doomed to failure. Many of those who fight death most desperately believe that nothing exists beyond this temporal world and life; they want to live forever, but as Benedict XVI noted in his encyclical on hope, "To continue living forever – endlessly – appears more like a curse than a gift. Death, admittedly, one would wish to postpone for as long as possible, but to live always, without end – this, all things considered, can only be monotonous and ultimately unbearable" (*Spe Salvi*, 10).

The Christian perspective is that, yes, death is evil and horrible, but death can only be conquered by death. For the Christian, the darkness of the grave is the passageway to resurrection and everlasting life. This is made possible by the death and resurrection of Christ, as expressed by St Paul in the epistle for Cycle A: "If the Spirit of the one who raised Jesus from the dead dwells in you, the one who raised Christ from the dead will give life to your mortal bodies also, through his Spirit dwelling in you" (*Rm* 8:11).

The story of the raising of Lazarus, a dear friend of Jesus, also heard in Cycle A, is one of the most poignant in the Gospels. It displays both the full humanity of Jesus: consider the simple power of the words "and Jesus wept" along with his full divinity. St Augustine captured the astounding wonder of that moment: "A man was raised up by him who made humankind." Death can only be overcome by the one who created life, who himself is Life itself. "I am the resurrection and the life," Jesus tells Martha, the grieving sister, "whoever believes in me, even if he dies, will live…" In the Gospel for Cycle B, Jesus delivers this bracing statement: "He who loves his life loses it, and he who hates his life in this world will keep it for eternal life" (*Jn* 12:25).

This stark challenge is perfectly matched by the overwhelming mercy offered to the woman caught in adultery (Cycle C), when Jesus declares, "Neither do I condemn you; go, and do not sin again" (*Jn* 8:11). During this final Sunday of Lent, take time in prayer to acknowledge that you are standing face to face with the righteous teacher and merciful judge. You know your sins; you are well aware of what you deserve. Further, you know that Jesus has not overlooked your sins. "Therefore the Lord did also condemn" insisted St Augustine "but condemned sins not the sinner." While rejecting your sin, he accepts you. He invites you to a radical life of discipleship, liberated from sin and free from being precariously balanced between accusation and damnation. he offers the fullness of life – that is, himself – perpetually and completely.

Such is the reality of the resurrection: Jesus died on the cross so that we might live; he gave so that we might be filled; he came down from heaven and then into the tomb so that we might be filled with divine life and ascend into glory: "Through him we have obtained access to this grace in which we stand and we rejoice in our hope of sharing the glory of God" (*Rm* 5:2). Amen!

Prayer

I love you, O my God, and my only desire is to love you until the last breath of my life. I love you, O my infinitely lovable God, and I would rather die loving you than live without loving you. I love you, Lord, and the only grace I ask is to love you eternally.... My God, if my tongue cannot say in every moment that I love you, I want my heart to repeat it to you as often as I draw breath.

St John Vianney, The Curé of Ars